"FORE" Your Family
FROM: Todd The Frog

This book is dedicated to my daughter Madeline

who created Todd the Frog when she was 3 years old

By: Robert "RT" Todd

Pictures by: Michael Schieffer

This book is family interactive:

Have the children find the hidden lady bug on each page

www.toddthefroggolf.com

5 4 3 2 1   2016 2015 2014 2013 2012

Library of Congress Cataloging-in-Publication Data

Library of Congress Control Number: 2012905079

ISBN-10 number 0615607314

ISBN-13 number 978-0-615-60731-3

Printed in the United States of America

Copyright Office record-TXu 1-790-761 effective March 6, 2012

Acknowledgements

My daughter Madeline
At the age of three she drew a picture of a frog in church and named him Todd the Frog.
I have to thank her and the Lord for giving me the inspiration to write this story.

Alice
My personal editor, advisor, consultant and most importantly, my friend, she and her family are golfers who believe spending time with your family and friends on the golf course is the best. She also introduced me to some talented people that helped with the book.

Michael
This talented illustrator was able to read my mind from across the country. I don't know how he did it. I have a feeling we have the golfing gods on our side. The pictures of the characters and their expressions plus the images of the golf course really make this book come alive.

Mom and Dad
They got me involved in the game of golf at an early age by spending quality time on the golf course together with me. Big hugs!!

Toni
My best friend's wife, she has shared her ideas with me on how to make the book appealing to children and their golfing families.

Turning Stone Resort and the Oneida Indian Nation
They have given me support on the book. The backdrop on each page of this book is from the Atunyote Golf Course at Turning Stone Resort. http://www.turningstone.com/golf/atunyote.php

The PGA of America
They have provided me with the services and knowledge to help in my search for a job closer to Madeline and support my interest in promoting family golf.

Down in the sunny meadow, a family of frogs lived happily in
a pond. They played hide-n-seek, Marco Polo and
leap frog all day long. Some frogs caught
flies with their long tongues.

One frog's name was Tad and he had the longest tongue. His friend Polly could jump very high. They both wanted to start a family of their own and that is how Todd the Frog was born.

One day when all the frogs were playing, they felt the ground rumble. A big tanker truck was coming to fill up with water from the pond.

Todd and Polly watched the truck while it pumped water out of the pond and noticed other big trucks and tractors coming towards the meadow.

This scared the family of frogs.

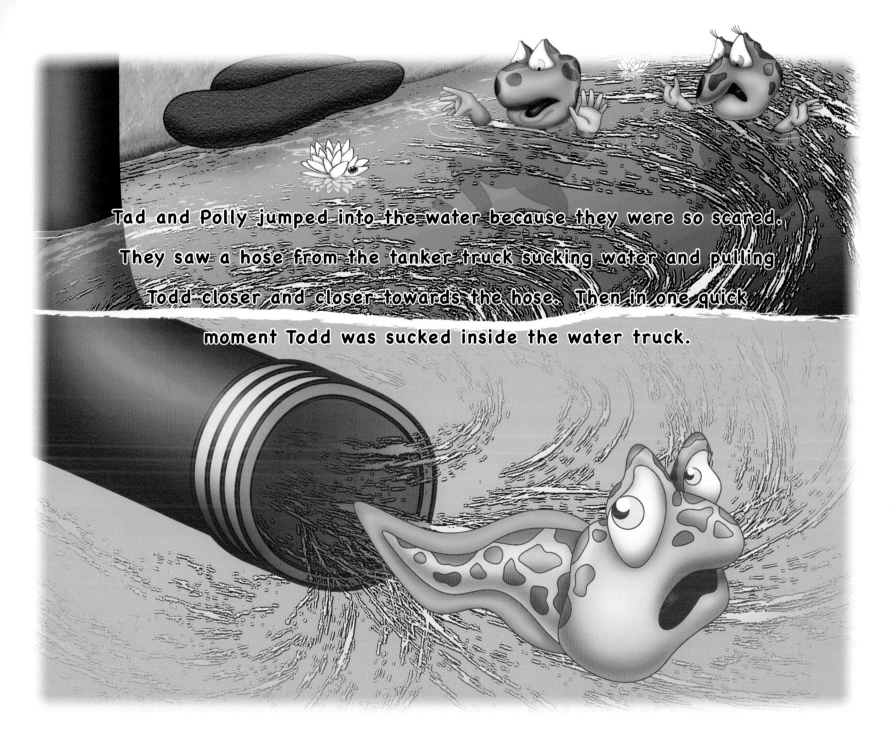

Tad and Polly jumped into the water because they were so scared. They saw a hose from the tanker truck sucking water and pulling Todd closer and closer towards the hose. Then in one quick moment Todd was sucked inside the water truck.

Polly and Tad chased the truck until it was out of sight. They returned to their home at the pond very sad. They were worried that they would never see their little tadpole, Todd again.

Todd was trapped in the dark and scary truck. Then the truck stopped and dumped all the water and Todd out. Todd found himself in a puddle beside a grassy field.

A few days went by and Todd noticed that he was growing legs.
Todd was turning into a frog! Soon he could leave the little puddle
and try to find his way back home to his family.

A few more days went by and Todd hopped out of the puddle confused. He did not know which way to go to begin his journey home. Suddenly a Wise Owl swooped down and tried to catch Todd.

Luckily, Todd leaped up just in time and the Wise Owl flew under him. The Wise Owl hit the ground and tumbled along the field to a stop.

Todd noticed the Wise Owl looked hurt and helped him up off the ground. When the Wise Owl got up, he thanked Todd for helping him and was sorry for trying to catch him. He asked Todd if he could help him in any way.

Todd told the Wise Owl how he was separated from his family and asked if he knew of the pond where his family lived. The Wise Owl did know and thought for a moment about how he could return Todd home safely.

The Wise Owl told Todd to follow the sound, "FORE" that was heard during the day because it sounded like a frog.

Maybe it was his family calling for him.

At that moment they both heard the sound, "FORE!"

Todd got excited and looked at the Wise Owl. The Wise Owl said,

"Head towards that noise and you will find your family!"

Todd then headed
in the direction of the sound.
He jumped into a stream
and swam until he came
to a pool of water.

At the pool of water, Todd saw a Busy Beaver

moving twigs and branches, building a dam.

The harder the Busy Beaver worked,

the faster the pool filled up with water.

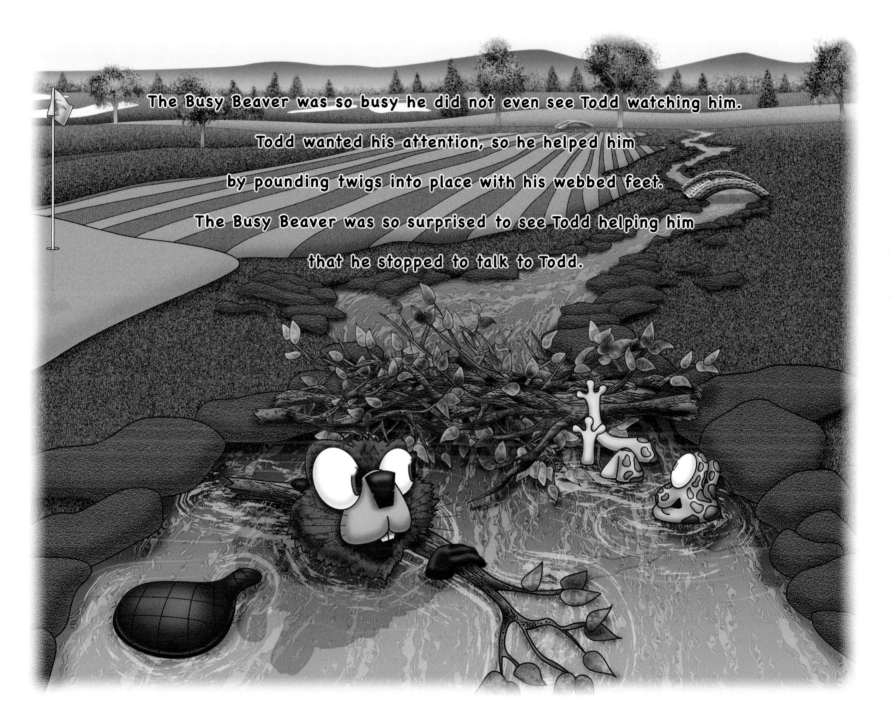

The Busy Beaver was so busy he did not even see Todd watching him.

Todd wanted his attention, so he helped him
by pounding twigs into place with his webbed feet.
The Busy Beaver was so surprised to see Todd helping him
that he stopped to talk to Todd.

Todd asked the Busy Beaver why he was building the dam and the Busy Beaver replied, "I am making a home and play area for my family."

The Busy Beaver and Todd played tag as the dam filled with water. They chased each other around until they were laughing so hard they had to stop. Then the Busy Beaver asked Todd, "Where are you going?" Todd told him how he was separated from his family and that his new friend the Wise Owl told him to follow the sound, "FORE."

The Busy Beaver pointed with his big tail and said,

"That is the direction where I hear the sound."

Just then Todd and the Busy Beaver heard,

"FORE!" in the distance

and it was louder than

before. Todd got very

excited and knew he was

getting closer to his family.

The Busy Beaver had an idea that would help his new friend Todd find his family faster. The Busy Beaver swam as quickly as he could towards the dam and in one blow he knocked the dam down. The water rushed out of the pond, sweeping Todd away. He looked back at the Busy Beaver, waving to say, "Thank you."

The rushing water flowed right into a lake near a putting green
where a Sly Fox was sitting. The Sly Fox asked Todd what happened.
Todd replied, "My friend the Busy Beaver
knocked down his dam to rush me to my family."

The Sly Fox asked Todd the Frog, "Where is your family?" Todd explained that he wasn't sure where his family was, but his new friend the Wise Owl told him to head towards the sound, "FORE."

The Sly Fox told Todd that he had sharp hearing and could pin point the location of the sound. Both Todd and the Sly Fox heard the sound, "FORE!" They looked at each other in surprise and headed in that direction.

Todd and the Sly Fox traveled
around the lake and approached a stone bridge. Halfway across
they were surprised to see a dog lying down on the bridge.
The Sly Fox looked at Todd and said, "Follow me." At that moment
the quick brown fox jumps over the lazy dog with Todd right behind.

Todd landed on the dog's tail and the dog started barking.
The PGA Golf Pro came out of the pro shop to see why the dog
was barking. He saw that the dog had a frog trapped against the wall of
the bridge. The Sly Fox ran away when he saw the Golf Pro coming.

The Golf Pro picked up Todd the Frog and carried him over to a nearby pond next to a putting green. "FORE"......."FORE!" The Golf Pro ducked and ran behind a tree to protect Todd and himself from being hit by a golfer's stray ball. "That is why they yell, "FORE!" to forewarn people," said the pro to the frog.

Todd had a sad look on his face when he realized that the noise that he had been following did not come from his family. Then Todd heard a similar noise and saw his family in the water swimming towards him! The Golf Pro gently put Todd in the water and said,

"This is where you belong."

Todd told his family about his journey and how he met three friends that helped him find his way back home. Just then, the Wise Owl, Busy Beaver and Sly Fox showed up to see if Todd made it home safely.

The foursome of Todd, the Wise Owl, Busy Beaver and Sly Fox learned to play golf and spent each day playing on the golf course. Every time they heard the sound "FORE," they laughed and thought of being with their families.

The End